Sacred and Romanesque
The First
Congregational Church
Jackson, Michigan

Kenneth Lingaur

Lingaur Preservation LLC
Clare, Michigan
2018

Sacred and Romanesque:
The First Congregational Church
Jackson, Michigan

Lingaur Preservation LLC
Clare, Michigan
www.lingaurpreservation.com
Printed in the U.S.A.

ISBN-13: 978-1-7322263-2-6
ISBN-10: 1-7322263-2-6

Cover design by Heather Todd
Postcard Image Courtesy of the First Congregational Church

To Dr. Ted Ligibel,
You counseled, mentored and inspired
hundreds of us to be preservationists.
It was fun to get my degree, but it is even
more fun working in the field.
Thank you for helping me
achieve my dream.

Table of Contents

Acknowledgements

Special thanks goes to Marilyn Guidinger who had the vision and perseverance to have her church, the First Congregational Church, listed on the National Register of Historic Places. Also, recognition goes other church historians: Robert Davey, Dewey West, Mr. and Mrs. Rood, and all the others who have chronicled the history of Jackson's First Congregational Church. Their many years of research and documentation have formed the basis for much of what is written here.

Thanks also go to Bob Christensen, former National Register coordinator of the Michigan State Historic Preservation Office. His recommendations on content and the final edits to the National Register of Historic Places Nomination were invaluable.

My wife, Sherrie, is also worthy of mention. Her encouragement and support on all of my projects are what keep me going.

Introduction

Since 1841, the First Congregational Church has held an important role in the history of Jackson, Michigan. The church is known for its stance on social justice issues which began with the anti-slavery and temperance movements in the 1800s. The church building, located at 120 North Jackson Street was listed on the National Register of Historic Places on July 10, 2017. The following significance statement gives the explanation for why the church was eligible for listing on the National Register.

The First Congregational Church of Jackson, Michigan meets Criteria C for listing on the National Register of Historic Places. It is one of the oldest Romanesque Revival church buildings in the state. The First Congregational Church is significant for its association with its designer Horatio Nelson White. The church is the only known example of Mr. White's work to exist in the State of Michigan. Horatio Nelson White was a prominent architect in the state of New York, particularly in the Syracuse area, during the early second half of the nineteenth century, and was a master of Romanesque Revival Style. The First Congregational Church is one of over 100 churches of his design. In addition, the stained glass windows in the church sanctuary are some of the oldest in the state.

As the author of the nomination, I took the text for this book from the National Register of Historic Places

Nomination. A nomination for the National Register of Historic Places is divided in two parts. The first part includes a current architectural description of building and a narrative of how the building changed over time. The second part describes how the building is historically significant. For this book I have presented the significance portion first and the descriptive part second.

The text here is a slightly edited version of the nomination. The information contained in boxes and all of the historic photographs were not included in the nomination. Enjoy reading about the history of Jackson's First Congregational Church building.

[4]

First Congregational Church
Jackson, Michigan

[5]

History of First Congregational Church Jackson, Michigan

On July 3, 1829, Horace Blackman, originally from Berkshire, New York, along with his guides Capt. Alexander Laverty and a Pottawatomie named Pewatum, crossed the Grand River where Jackson Street and Trail Street currently intersect, and became the first white settler in Jackson County. At the time Michigan was only a territory, and would not attain statehood until 1837.

In the years following Blackman's settlement, a village called Jacksonburgh would begin to develop. The village of Jacksonburgh would be officially platted in January 1830, and later that year would obtain a population of 123. The county of Jackson was organized in 1832 with Jacksonburgh being named the county seat. That same year the territorial road known as the St. Joseph Road was extended from Ann Arbor to the Grand River into Jacksonburgh. The name of the village would be shortened to Jackson in 1838.

The first religious meeting in the village was held in June 1830 at the home of J. W. Bennett, but was not officiated by a clergyman. An unknown Baptist minister preached the first sermon in the village on the evening of January 26, 1831. The following evening the Methodist circuit preacher the Rev. E. H. Pilcher gave the first of what would become regular services in the town of Jackson. In September of the same year the Methodist church became the first organized religious congregation in the village. The Catholics were next to establish a church presence in 1836.

The Presbyterian Church in Jackson was organized in June 1837 with thirteen members by the Rev. Marcus Harrison. The church held services in a wood framed building they leased called the "Session House." The Rev. Harrison and many of the first members were originally Congregationalists before they moved from the

Session House, date unknown
The building was used not only for public gatherings but also as a residence. It was located at the corner of South Jackson and Washington Streets.
Photograph from the First Congregational Collection

eastern part of the country. The union between Presbyterian and Congregational Churches in the western frontier was a common practice. The "Plan of Union" was adopted by the General Assembly of the Presbyterian Church and the General Association of Connecticut in 1801. The Plan of Union provided a means for competing Presbyterian and Congregational churches in the same community, with relatively the same beliefs, but differing in their form of church governance, to form one church. This unity combined resources and increased the chances of the church's survival where resources may be limited (Goodykoontz, pg. 149).

In the early days of Michigan's history, until the late 1830s, the union of Presbyterian and Congregational Churches usually resulted in the formation of a Presbyterian church. However, the late 1830s saw a change in the beliefs of the Presbyterian leadership that would drive congregations away from the Presbyterian form of church government to the Congregational form. These changes were mainly in the method of church discipline and the adoption of a pro-slavery stance. The church in Jackson was one of the early churches in Michigan to leave the Presbytery. The church in Marshall left in 1838, Grand Rapids, Hudson and Vermontville in 1839, and Jackson along with Union City, Grass Lake and Almont in 1840. The cycle of Presbyterian churches changing over to Congregational churches would increase and continue into the 1850s (Taylor).

On March 6, 1841 the Rev. Harrison along with fifty-eight members subscribed to the articles of faith and covenant of the Congregational Church, while a small portion of the original members continued their association with the Presbyterian Church.

The Congregational Church immediately began making plans for constructing a new house of worship. In April 1841 plans were drawn up for a new brick building measuring forty by sixty feet, with a Greek temple portico on the front of the building. The church was located on the west end of the Public Square north of the present West Michigan Avenue. The Public Square consisted of two city lots located at each of the corners of the intersection of the present West Michigan Avenue and Jackson Street. This would be the first brick church constructed in Jackson.

Work on the building began in 1841. By 1842, with all the church's funds expended, work came to a standstill. During the construction of the new building the church continued to meet in the Session House. In early 1843 the Session House was sold to new owners who converted it to a carpenter shop. The Congregational Church would then share the use of the Presbyterian Church building which was known as the "Pepper Box" for a few months. The Presbyterian Church disbanded in June 1843 and united with the Congregational Church. With this union the Congregationalists acquired ownership of the building which was formerly owned by the Presbyterian Church. The Pepper Box was sold to the Methodist Church for the amount of $350.00, and the money was put toward the completion of the Congregational Church's new brick building.

With the sale of The Pepper Box building, the Congregational Church moved their services to "Porter's

(Continued on page 12)

Congregational Church building, 1844-1860
Photograph from the First Congregational Church Collection

"Many stories are told of organizing pastor, Marcus Harrison, who on week-days operated a farm and saw-mill at Spring Arbor. His outspoken sermons on the evils of intemperance and slavery made bitter enemies. They stole the bell from the Session House. They cut off his horse's mane and tail. But the members continued to gather in the Session House, and each Sunday the mutilated horse jogged in from Spring Arbor. Finally, when Mr. Harrison was warned that a plot had been made to kill him he hid for several days in a swamp near Blackstone Street, but he returned to preach.

Meanwhile a site for a church building had been purchased from S. H. Kimball on the west side of the north-west square – one of the four squares originally plotted to form a village park at the intersection of Jackson and Main Streets. Pastor Harrison, working alone with his ox team, leveled a hill on that side of the square and excavated a cellar. He engaged workmen to raise the black walnut frame. When they refused to work without free whiskey, Mr. Harrison appealed to two other pastors. The next Monday the frame was raised by volunteers from the three congregations. This was the first public building in Jacksonburgh to be raised without free whiskey.

Since plaster was not available nearer than Grand Rapids, S. B. Stowell drove there with his ox team and brought back a load as his donation. The trip took more than two weeks. (Such devotion reminds one of the stories that come back from a mission field these days.)

The building was completed in 1845. It was a brick veneer with a porch and blinds. The blinds were the gift of Frederick Kirtland. The old Session House bell had never been found, but a good new bell was bought. The town used it on week-days to announce that court was in session at Bronson Hall, and doubtless in return for this accommodation the town placed a clock in the tower, showing four faces. When the present church building was finished the bell was transferred to it and is still in use. There was no room for the clock which was moved to the tower of the old Methodist Church.

The Congregationalists held services in their first building for sixteen years. When they needed a larger place for worship, this one was sold to the Jewish congregation for a Temple, and later to the Christian Scientists. The quaint and beautiful little church was torn down when the Consumer's Power building was erected."

Excerpt from the *Centennial Program 1841-1941*
First Congregational Church, Jackson, Michigan

Hall" located on the south side of the Public Square on the east side of Jackson Street. They met there until the completion of their brick building in the autumn of 1844.

The village of Jackson would steadily grow through the 1830s and 1840s. The 1838 *Gazetteer of Michigan* lists the population of Jackson at four hundred, with seventy-five dwellings. The following year the population had grown to one thousand with two hundred buildings and eighty more stores and dwellings underway. Jackson was serviced by two railroads, the Michigan Central (1841) and the Michigan Southern (1858). It was incorporated as a city in 1857.

With the growth of the city also came the growth of the Congregational Church. The year 1847, saw the church membership grow by ninety-five members. It would go down as one of the largest accessions of membership for a single year in the church's history. By mid-century, the church membership would grow to 222. The church began discussions on how to expand their building. However, in October 1858 the church's trustees were directed to find a suitable site for the construction of a new building (History of Jackson and First Congregational Church summarized from DeLand 202-210, and *History of Jackson County Michigan*, 483-495).

The Rev. William Dada became the new leader of the Jackson Congregational Church in June 1858. Under his leadership, Joseph E. Beebe, George F. Rice, F. Woodbury, N. S. Hubell, G. Thompson Gridley and Phillip Thurber were appointed to a building committee. In December 1858, the committee was authorized to purchase two city lots on the north side of the Public Square from Fidus Livermore for a sum not to exceed five thousand dollars (DeLand, 208-209). By early 1859, they had accepted architectural plans from Horatio Nelson White of Syracuse, New York, and had also hired James Morwick, also of Syracuse, to construct the new church building. It is known that several, if not all the committee members originated from the New England area, but it cannot be determined if any had a connection to Mr. White or the Syracuse area. However, it is known that the Rev. Dada was from Otisco, New York, a town about ten miles from Syracuse.

It was not an unusual practice for a congregation in Michigan to hire an architect from out of state. Several churches in Michigan from the late 1840s to 1870s hired architects from the eastern United States. Calvin Otis, an architect from Buffalo, New York, designed Mariner's Church, Detroit (1849), St. Paul's Episcopal Church, Jackson (1850-1853), and St. Paul's Episcopal Church, Detroit (1852). Charles Marsh from Rochester, New York designed the First Congregational Church, Charlotte (1872-1876) and the First Congregational Church, Romeo (1876-1877). Another architect, Sidney Mason Stone from New Haven, Connecticut designed the church building for the Whitewater Congregational Society (1866), near present day Williamsburg.

Horatio Nelson White was born in Middleton, New Hampshire in 1814. He moved with his parents to Andover, Massachusetts, where he worked as a builder and carpenter. Before coming to Syracuse, New York in 1843, White spent a short time in New York City. He would soon leave for California during the Gold Rush where he continued to work as a builder and to a smaller degree a designer. Mr. White spent three years in California before returning to Syracuse in 1853, when he began work as an architect. His most well-known building was the Onondaga County Court House in Syracuse, which is of a Romanesque Revival style built in 1857. He also designed the Oswego County Court House (1859), the Chemung County Courthouse (1861), and the Jefferson County Courthouse (1865). All of these courthouses were of similar design to the Onondaga Court House. Mr. White would later design the Hall of Language (1873), the first building on the campus of Syracuse University. He

Horatio Nelson White
1814-1892

was also responsible for the design of over one hundred churches, including the Church of the Messiah (1853), the Plymouth Congregational Church (1858-1859), and the Grace Episcopal Church (1877), all within Syracuse. He also designed an unknown number of residences, and numerous commercial and governmental buildings in the Syracuse area and New York State Armory buildings of Syracuse, Dunkirk, and Ballston Spa. A 1988 book by Elinore T. Horning describes Horatio Nelson White as titled "The Man Who Changed the Face of Syracuse (Parsons and Horning).

In designing the Congregational Church in Jackson, it is likely the building committee, along with the Rev. Dada and Horatio Nelson White consulted the *Book of Plans for Churches and Parsonages*. This book, which was written in 1853, was a guide to Congregational Churches in America on the design of new church buildings. The book contained thirty pages of text followed by eighteen designs by architects: Henry Austin, William Backus, David R. Brown, Henry Cleveland, T. Reeve, James Renwick, Sidney M. Stone, Richard Upjohn, Joseph C. Wells, and Gervase Wheeler. Although it is not known who the actual author was, it was written in consultation with businessmen Simeon B. Chittenden and Henry C. Bowen, both founding members of the Church of the Pilgrim in Brooklyn, New York, and three Congregationalist ministers Richard Salter Storrs, George Barrell Cheever, and Nathaniel Egleston.

In making suggestions on church design the *Book of Plans for Churches and Parsonages* favored the Romanesque style as the preferred style for construction, but plans in other styles were also provided. Much of the preference to the Romanesque style was a rejection of the Gothic style with its pointed stained glass windows, side chapels, elaborate details and narrow plan. Protestants sometimes associated the Gothic style to what it called "popery." They considered the Gothic style to be inappropriate to their less liturgical practices. In addition, the Gothic style was considered an expensive style to build, with all its elaborate ornamentation.

In choosing building materials the *Book of Plans for Churches and Parsonages* encouraged the use of stone for its natural look and permanence. However, brick would become the more popular building material. When brick and wood were chosen the honesty of the material was advocated. Honesty of material meant that brick or wood should not be made to look like any other material except its own. However, brick could be painted if it was not meant to look like stone. In addition interior walls were to be painted in soft neutral colors, and woodwork was meant to be stained and varnished.

The construction of the Jackson Congregational Church began in 1859. The completed church was dedicated on October 18, 1860. The September 1, 1859 issue of *The*

American Citizen had the following description of the church building under construction:

Architecture of the church is to be of the Norman Gothic style, a trifle modernized in some points. The whole size of the church proper is 88 by 62 feet; attached to this and accessible by doors on each side of the Pulpit is the Session and Sabbath School room, which is 60 by 26 feet. In front of the church is a porch 12¼ by 6¼ feet; 18 feet high, finished by carved key stone and ornamented cornice. The floor of the porch is a single solid stone, 13 feet long; 7 feet wide and 8 inches thick. This stone is now on the ground and was occupied by the speakers as their platform. On each side of the porch rises two towers of brick and stone, 15 feet square. The Dwarf tower on the west, to be finished with Cupola roof and carved finial, is 75 feet high. The east tower is to be finished with four gables and eight carved finials, and is to be 100 feet high. The front steps are to be of solid stone, 9 feet long, 16 inches wide, 8 inches thick; the door sill 9 by 2½ feet, 8 inches thick of Joliet stone. There will be a large set of tribble windows in front over the porch, stone sills, half circle heads, two sets of double windows and the two four-foiled windows in each tower. The foundation walls are all four feet thick, laid of dressed stone, each bearing point strengthened by

[17]

strong inverted arches. The basement is six feet in the clear. The walls of the main building are 31 feet high, the roof gable 18, making a total of 49 feet as the height of the church. There are to be six windows on each side, 4 by 18 feet, arched tops, to be set with stained diamond glass in colored borders. Between each window is a heavy buttress with double offsets, corniced with moulded stone. The main cornice is to be of wood and enriched with cobble brackets. The inside and ceiling is to be stucco and frescoed with antique mouldings and cornices. There is to be an orchestra over the front vestibule. The pulpit is of good size, not extravagantly ornamental, and to be of solid oak. There will be 156 slips; a row of wall slips on each side, slightly diagonal to face the pulpit and two tiers of body slips. The main aisles are four feet and the side aisles are three feet in the clear. The slips are to be of panel work, with carved arms, to be constructed of Butternut wood, varnished and upholstered throughout. Each slip will seat six persons, thus furnishing seats for 936 persons without crowding. The conference room is to be finished in a plain and substantial manner and will be very convenient connecting as it does by two doors with the main edifice and the street. The whole building is to be warmed by two large furnaces in the basement of the main building. The name of the Architect is

H. N. White, Syracuse, N. Y., and the Builder is Mr. James Morwick of the same city. Both of these men are able and experienced in their profession, as both design and work already show. Plymouth Church in Syracuse and the Baptist Church in Eldridge, N. Y., were designed and built by them. The total cost of the Church when completed is estimated at twenty thousand dollars.

As mentioned above James Morwick of Syracuse, New York was the builder of the Congregational Church. Little is known about Mr. Morwick. He is listed in both the 1855 and 1859 Syracuse city directories as a carpenter and building contractor. The 1860 census lists him as fifty-two years of age, and his occupation as Master Carpenter. The 1862 Syracuse city directory does not include a listing for him.

"The present building was erected in 1859. It was dedicated in 1860, at the time when the war clouds were gathering over the land, and it was from this new church that the Jackson Greys held their farewell service when they left for the scene of the fighting. The Jackson Greys, being a military club under the Captaincy of W. M. Bennett. Under Lieutenant, later General Withington, they were the first Michigan Company to volunteer."

Excerpt from the *Centennial Program 1841-1941*
First Congregational Church, Jackson, Michigan

Upon moving into their new building, the Congregational Church sold its former building to the Beth Israel congregation. They occupied the building until sometime between 1899 and 1907, when the First Church of Christ Scientists acquired it. The building is not shown on the 1930 Sanborn Map.

The decade of the 1860s continued to be a time of positive growth for the Jackson Congregational Church. The year 1866 was the largest year of growth in the history of the church with acceptance of one hundred and fifty new members. As the result of a mission school, which the church operated for a number of years on the east side of the city, the Second Congregational Church was organized in 1867. Another eighty-nine new members were received to the now First Congregational Church in 1869.

By 1871, the need for more room in the church was evident. The problem was not the sanctuary which could seat over 900 people, but the lack of a meeting hall and Sunday school rooms. The desire for the First Congregational Church to expand its building followed a general pattern with other Protestant churches in the middle to late nineteenth century. In the past churches were content to use their auditoriums for most of their functions. By mid-century the desire for separate rooms to accommodate smaller gatherings deemed too small for the auditorium was becoming popular. The "Session and Sabbath School room" to the north of the auditorium in the First Congregational church originally filled this purpose. The post-Civil War era also saw a rapid expansion of the Sunday school institution, and an increased need for rooms to accommodate those classes. In addition, rooms for

First Congregational Church, in center of drawing, circa 1868
From the Bird's-eye View of the City of Jackson, Michigan
A. Ruger and Chicago Lithography Co., Chicago, Illinois

parlors, chapels, and other functions were growing in demand.

The difficulty for the First Congregational Church was where to build an addition. The church was located close to two adjoining streets on its north and east sides, by a city park on the south, and a newly constructed parsonage on the west. The plan was to raise the building and construct a new ground story that would fulfill their space needs beneath the existing building. This method of expansion was not uncommon for Protestant churches of the time. New churches were being constructed with the Sunday schools rooms designed for the ground story and an auditorium above, but existing churches were also being raised, like the First Congregational Church, and new ground stories added beneath to fill the need for smaller rooms.

To build below the First Congregational Church, the building had to be raised off its foundation and the six foot tall basement made higher. The job of raising the building was performed by Hollingsworth & Coughlan of Chicago. James Hollingsworth originally partnered with James Brown, and their Chicago company began raising and sometimes moving buildings starting in 1858. Hollingsworth and Brown were pioneers in the business of raising stone, brick and iron buildings. Most of their early work was confined to the Chicago area where they raised buildings to improve the health conditions of the city. Chicago was a marshy area with frequent outbreaks of typhoid fever and dysentery. The raising of buildings and in some cases entire streets of buildings allowed for the marshes to be filled in and proper sewage systems to be installed. By the time Hollingsworth & Coughlan came to

Jackson in 1871 they had developed a reputation of being the premier company in the Midwest to safely raise a building without damage to the structure. Their work extended from the Rocky Mountains to the Atlantic Ocean and as far south as New Orleans.

The work of raising the First Congregational Church started on July 5, 1871. Eight days later the local newspaper reported, "The foundations have been pretty well knocked out from under the Congregational Church, and it will be ready to be raised soon" (*Jackson Daily Citizen*, July 13, 1871). About one week later the paper wrote "The Congregational Church will be raised tomorrow morning…The timbers have all been placed in position, and the building rests upon the screws. If they can be obtained, forty men will be employed in raising the building" (*Jackson Daily Citizen*, July 21, 1871). The process of raising the building was explained the following day: "The preliminaries having been all arranged, the work of raising the Congregational Church commenced this morning with quite a large force. Every precaution has been taken to prevent damage to the walls, and as far as we are able to judge, none will occur. The *modus operandi* in working the jacks after they are in positon under the timbers which supports the walls is very simple. Each of the men engaged attends to a certain number of screws, and at the signal from a policeman's whistle, gives each a certain number of turns, and then waits for another signal. when the operation is repeated; and so on till the screw is run out, when new blocking and jacks are placed in position, and the operation is resumed. There are six hundred jacks under the building at one time. Today it has been raised about a foot and a half; but it will

First Congregational Church, 1871
During Raising of Building
Photograph from the First Congregational Church Collection

take all of next week to complete the job, as a great deal of time is consumed in changing the screws" (*Jackson Daily Citizen*, July 22, 1871). The raising of the church to the required eight feet was completed on July 28, 1871.

With the building now raised the next step was the masonry work. The *Jackson Daily Citizen* was giving several reports each week on the progress of the construction, and filed this report on July 29: "The church having been raised the required distance, the mason work was commenced this morning by Mr. Hugh Richards, the contractor. It will be carried forward as rapidly as possible" (*Jackson Daily Citizen*, July 29, 1871).

A series of three articles were published in a nine-day span in mid-August detailing the progress of the brick layers: "The brick work upon the Congregational Church is nearly far enough advanced for the removal of the screws employed in raising it. The ground is to be graded up in front for the new entrance, and stone steps laid a portion of the way up" (*Jackson Daily Citizen*, August 15, 1871). "This morning the removal of the screws and beams upon which the Congregational Church rested was commenced. They will be removed a few at a time as fast as possible until the job is completed" (*Jackson Daily Citizen*, August 18, 1871). "The last beam will be removed from under the Congregational Church tomorrow, and it is expected that the building will be ready for resumption of services by the time [the Rev.] Mr. Hough's return, which is to be on or before the 3rd of next month. The preliminary work upon the basement has already been commenced. The new part will be cut up as follows: Off the front end will be a furnace room fourteen by forty feet, then back of that will come the chapel, forty feet square, still further in the rear is the church parlor, twenty-eight by forty feet, and in the rear of the whole is a room which will ultimately be used for an engine in case of the adoption of steam for warming purposes. Off the west side will be taken three rooms each twenty by twenty eight feet. They will be used for bible classes and prayer meeting rooms, etc." (*Jackson Daily Citizen*, August 23, 1871).

The *Jackson Daily Citizen* gave the following recap of the construction:

> The last beam has been taken from under the Congregational Church and the last brick has been laid. The workmen are today engaged in shoveling the dirt out of the basement, and in laying the stone platform in front, up to which the ground is to be graded.
>
> Now that the most difficult part of the work has been completed it is befitting that we speak of it, and tell how it is done. The raising of the building done by Messr. Hollingsworth & Co. of Chicago has been chronicled as it progressed and commented on. The mason work executed by Mr. Hugh Richards of this city, architect and builder, has been only casually alluded to. No one unacquainted with mason work can fully appreciate the difficulties in working around the timbers and beams in such a job as this, but not withstanding all these Mr. Richards has done an excellent piece of workmanship – the best according to Mr. Hollingsworth that the firm who raised the church ever has done for them.

First Congregational Church, circa mid-1870s
After Completion of Addition
Photograph from the First Congregational Church Collection

This considering the source is no insignificant praise.

Mr. Richards, who has only been in Jackson about two years has erected some of the finest blocks in the city. He has built the Hurd House Block, Withington's Block, Reynold's Block at the corner of Main and Mechanic Streets, the Central Block, and the Jackson City Water Works. He was also the builder of the new hotel recently erected at Eaton Rapids. Mr. Richards is now engaged upon the new store in process of erection for Alfonso Bennett Esq. near the Methodist Church..." (*Jackson Daily Citizen*, August 30, 1871).

By the end of September, with the Church basement not yet finished, the newspaper reported: "The Congregational Society has not decided yet whether to borrow money and finish off the basement of the church this fall or allow it to remain until next spring. A meeting of the trustees will decide the matter next week" (*Jackson Daily Citizen*, September 27, 1871). The trustees at that meeting voted to go ahead and finish the building immediately instead of waiting until the spring (*Jackson Daily Citizen*, October 7, 1871).

The entryway was the next addition to the First Congregational Church building. The current entryway was constructed in 1895 (*Jackson Daily Citizen*, June 19, and September 9, 1895). This entailed the elimination of the front steps and the construction of the entrance at ground level. The vestibule with the dark oak stairway was added, along with the four lowest stained glass windows on the façade. The two side entrances at the south end of the sanctuary were fixed closed in favor of the center entrance. New stained glass windows were installed in the second story of the entryway.

The interior of the church building has gone through a number of modifications to its decorations. This seemed to happen about every twenty years. The years in which these changes took place and the modifications are described as follows:

1880 From DeLand page 210

> The sanctuary is re-frescoed, new carpeting, chandeliers, and pulpit furniture added at a cost of about $2,000.00.

1899 From *Jackson Citizen Patriot*, October 14 and 16, 1899

> The sanctuary and Sunday school rooms are redecorated, new carpeting and electric lighting installed, and steam pipes overhauled, at a cost of $2,400.00.

1923 From *Jackson Daily Citizen*, October 7, 1923

> The auditorium of the church has been entirely re-decorated and furnished with all new lighting fixtures during the summer. The pews, pulpit, furniture, wainscoting and all the woodwork have been stained in walnut. The floor covering has

First Congregational Church, in center of drawing, 1881
From the Panoramic View of the City of Jackson, Michigan 1881
A. Ruger, J. Stoner, and Beck & Pauli, Madison, Wis.

been replaced and the pew cushions have been entirely re-covered.

The walls have been given a two-tone finish with a red and green stencil above the wainscoting. The rosettes in the ceiling and the moulding have been finished in gold and green bringing out the full beauty of the architecture. The ceiling itself, the arches over the windows, the arch over the organ recess and the gallery arches have all been finished in ivory.

Indirect Lighting System

The new lighting fixtures are of hammered Swedish iron with an Etruscan finish mixed with touches of polychrome. The glassware in them is

First Congregational Church, on right, circa 1900
Photograph from the First Congregational Church Collection

First Congregational Church, circa 1905
Photograph from the First Congregational Church Collection

all ivory-etched, made in a mold designed particularly for the First Congregational Church. The fixtures are also designed unique to the local church. There are no exposed light sources, thus preventing any glare but allowing an adequate illumination for the entire auditorium. Light will be provided by 106 lamps.

The platform has been extended into the auditorium four feet to give sufficient room for a large chorus choir. A new grand piano has been installed to supplement the organ in chorus work.

The church is Gothic in architecture and the subdued effect obtained in the re-decorated interior gives an atmosphere of rest and peace, probably unexcelled in any Jackson church. An air of an old European cathedral pervades the auditorium since its renovation, offering the best possible background for Divine worship.

All the materials for the work were furnished through Jackson firms and practically all Jackson labor used.

1945 From *Jackson Citizen Patriot*, November 3, 1945

First Congregational Church members and friends will meet Sunday morning in the main auditorium or sanctuary which has been closed four weeks while being repainted and redecorated. The church has just completed improvements that cost upward of $6,000.00.

The ceiling of the auditorium has been painted a deep blue and the walls an antique pink and mellow colors have been employed throughout, in keeping with the age and dignity of the building erected in 1859 and enlarged in 1871.

Other portions of the building have been repainted and redecorated, and the improvements included new furnace equipment with stoker and automatic controls. Some work was also done on the outside of the edifice and at the parsonage.

After fifteen years of being unused because of safety issues, the bell and the belfry are repaired.

"This church building has been refurbished from time to time through memorial funds contributed by various persons... Some of these improvements made in the church have been:

south entrance way to the church by the family of the Rev. William Steensma, who was serving as the pastor of the church when he died December 28, 1925;

elevator in the north entrance way dedicated September 30, 1973, as a memorial to Norman C. Lyon and Arthur S. Wilder;

the oil painting "Christ and the Fisherman" by Zimmerman... given in memory of Blanche Bullock Hirschman in 1936;

the sculpture of an angel singing with [cherubim] and [seraphim], sculpted by Robert Frost...given by the Hirschman Sunday School Class in memory of long-time teacher, Blanche Bullock Hirschman;
and

a silver tea service...donated by Mary Kassick who, when she died on March 21, 1915, was the last charter member of the church."

Excerpt from the *Bicentennial Program, 1976*
First Congregational Church, Jackson, Michigan

Stained Glass Windows

Although it is not known who designed and made the original stained glass windows for the First Congregational Church, they are without a doubt original to the building. They fit the description of the windows from the 1859 newspaper article describing the soon to be built church, "There are to be six windows on each side, 4 by 18 feet, arched tops, to be set with stained diamond glass in colored borders" (*The American Citizen*, September 1, 1859). Their age of more than 150 years makes them some of the oldest stained glass windows in the State of Michigan.

Original Stained Glass, 2017
*Photograph from
the Author's Collection*

Stained Glass Window, 2017
Located in 1895 Addition
Photograph from the Author's Collection

"Originally one reached the auditorium steps on the outside of the building and entered the basement by grade door facing Jackson Street. On rainy days between church and Sunday School a procession of dripping umbrellas came down the steps and around the corner. Fortunately there was room to install steps inside the tower and the entrance was changed to its present form [1895]."

Excerpt from the *Centennial Program 1841-1941*
First Congregational Church, Jackson, Michigan

Organs

The church has had two organs during its history. The first was acquired in 1866 from the Hook Brothers of Boston, and was purchased at a price of $3,500.00. After the church was constructed in 1860 the music had always been performed from the gallery at the rear of the church. When the Hook organ was purchased the plan was to place it behind the pulpit instead of up in the gallery. To accomplish this the large lecture room located behind the pulpit was converted to an organ loft, with additional space from the room used for the pastor's study (DeLand, page 209).

Hook Organ, circa 1920s
Photograph from the First Congregational Church Collection

The Hook organ served the church until 1926 when it was replaced by the current Casavant organ. The Hook organ was sold to the Congregational Church in Hart, Michigan. The Casavant organ was purchased from the firm of Casavant Freres, of Saint-Hyacinthe, Province of Quebec, Canada. The J. A. Herbert & Son Company in Detroit installed the organ (Davey).

"Within other alterations took place. At first there was no choir loft. A prayer meeting room was partitioned off behind the pulpit, and the choir sat in the balcony. After the minister "lined out" the hymns, the congregation turned and "faced the music." During the days of crinoline petticoats, the ladies found the turning process difficult. In response to their vigorous protests the congregation decided to face the front. It was still led in songs from the rear until the pipe-organ was purchased in [1866] and the choir loft took the place of the prayer meeting room.

The present pipe organ, a memorial gift to the church was first used in public worship on September 5, 1926, when the Reverend A. R. Brown preached his first sermon as pastor of the church. The organ was given as a memorial to Henry H. Bingham, Amelia Wells Bingham, [and] Mary Wells Bingham, by the daughter Florence Bingham Sumner, and the grandson Edward Alleyne Sumner."

Excerpt from the *Centennial Program 1841-1941*
First Congregational Church, Jackson, Michigan

Bell

The bell which is located currently in the east tower was acquired in 1846 for the Congregational Church when it constructed its brick building in the 1840s. It was made by the Andrew Meneely Foundry in West Troy, New York in 1846. When the current church building was constructed the bell from the 1840s building was removed to this building. From historic photographs the bell has been located in a number of places through its history. For a time between 1871 and 1895 the bell was located on the exterior of the southeast corner of the east tower (see photograph on page 27). Between 1895 and 1900 the bell was located on the exterior of the southeast corner of the west tower (see photograph on page 31). Since about the turn of the twentieth century the bell has been located within the east tower.

First Congregational Church Bell, 2017
Photograph from the Dennis Richard Collection

Christian Education Building

The mid-twentieth century saw the need for once again expanding the church building. This time a shortage of space for the new addition was not a problem. The parsonage on the west side of the church was removed sometime between 1945 and 1950, and replaced with a parking lot. The new modern addition was constructed as a Christian Education Wing, and provided classrooms, offices for the pastor, assistant pastor and secretary, along with a conference room, restrooms and storage areas. To save space and money, the classrooms were built with doorways connecting one to another instead of using a

Christian Education Wing, 2017
Addition to west elevation, 1960-1961
Photograph from the Author's Collection

hallway. The addition was built with a proposed budget of $140,000.00 (*Jackson Citizen* Patriot, June 25, 1960).

The addition was designed by local architect and church member Claude Dewitt Sampson. Claude Sampson graduated with his undergraduate degree in architecture from the University of Michigan in 1930. The following year he studied at the L'Ecole de Beaux Arts in Paris, France, where he specialized in ecclesiastic architecture in the Atelier Gromort. Mr. Sampson then earned his graduate degree in architecture from the University of Michigan in 1933. After working for a number of firms Claude Sampson opened his own firm in Jackson in 1948. Buildings designed by Claude Sampson include: W. S. Butterfield Residence, Jackson, MI (1952), Woodworth Elementary School, Leslie, MI (1953), Mrs. B. F. Green Residence, Hillsdale, MI (1953), Jackson County Library & Sanctuary Remodel (1954), First Baptist Church Addition, Jackson, MI (1954), Hanover-Horton School, Horton, MI (1954), and the Woodland Cemetery Chapel, Jackson (1975).

"Down through the years, events witnessed within these walls were not merely of local significance. Here on May 17, 1842 the Jackson Association of Congregational Churches was formed. Also, pursuant to a call issued by that body, the "General Association of Congregational Churches and Ministers of Michigan" was organized here on October 11, 1842. Here on July 2, 1847, the Dorcas Society was organized, this being the first women's organization in the church... In 1903 the Junior Dorcas Society was organized... It first met in homes, but in 1912 this church became its meeting place. Both of these organizations have performed extensive local social welfare accomplishments."

Excerpt from the *Bicentennial Program 1976*
First Congregational Church, Jackson, Michigan

Historic Plaques

The First Congregational Church was designated as a Historic Site in 1977 by the Jackson Historic District Commission. This plaque, located near the entryway of the building, commemorates that designation.

FIRST CONGREGATIONAL CHURCH

This monumental Romanesque Revival church was erected in 1859 according to plans by architect Horatio N. White of Syracuse, New York. It is this congregation's third church. In 1871 the building was raised eight feet to accommodate lower-level classrooms. In September 1861, on the eve of departing for duty in the Civil War, the "Jackson Blair Cadets" and the Jackson County Rifles gathered with their families in the crowded sanctuary. At Detroit's Fort Wayne the troops joined the Eighth and Ninth Michigan infantries respectively. Beginning in the 1840s with the antislavery movement, the congregation actively participated in social reform -- most notably the temperance and civil rights crusades.

This plaque has been located on the southeast corner of the building since the First Congregational Church was listed as a Michigan State Historic Site in 1987.

Commemorating the listing of the church on the National Register of Historic Places in 2017, this plaque was added to the exterior of the entryway in 2018.

Photographs of plaques from the Author's Collection

Romanesque Revival Style

The Romanesque Revival style, sometimes known as "Norman" or "Lombard" styles, was popular in American architecture from the 1840s to the 1870s. The style was adopted by architects who were influenced by German architecture known as Rundbogenstil, or translated into English as "Round-Arch Style." Rundbogenstil became popular in Germany during the early 1800s by architects Leo von Klenze and Karl Friedrich Schinkel. The American Romanesque Revival style incorporated design elements from Germany, Northern Italy, and England. The first building designed in this style in America is considered the Church of Pilgrims, in Brooklyn Heights, Brooklyn, designed by Richard Upjohn (1844-1846). Another early building in this style is the Smithsonian Institute in Washington D.C., designed by James Renwick Jr. (1847-1851).

The number of surviving buildings in this style is not a good indicator of the popularity of the Romanesque Revival style. Architectural historian Carroll

Church of the Pilgrims
From
"The 'Book of Plans' and the Early Romanesque Revival in the United States"

Meeks was of the opinion that between 1846 and 1876 the majority of American buildings were constructed in the round-arch style. Of the hundreds of buildings built in the style, many were demolished. In New York City, buildings built in the 1840s were razed by the 1860s, as were many post-Civil War buildings. Cities such as Springfield, Syracuse, and Detroit also experienced a loss of Romanesque Revival buildings, but not at a rate found in New York City (Meeks).

The Romanesque Revival style as a design for churches was more popular in Protestant denominations than in Catholic. Catholic churches tended to be designed in the Gothic style, but some examples can be found in the Romanesque Revival style. Some early examples of the Romanesque Revival style in the Detroit area included the Tabernacle Baptist Church (1859-1860) on the corner of Washington and Clifford Streets, the First Baptist Church (1859-1863) on the corner of Fort and Griswold Streets, and the Westminster Presbyterian Church (1860-1861) located on the east side of Washington Street between State and Grand River (Farmer). All of these churches no longer exist.

Protestant examples of the style within Michigan that still exist are as follows: St. Paul's Episcopal Church, Jackson (1850-1853), First Presbyterian Church, Coldwater (1866-1869), First Free Will Baptist Church, Hillsdale (1867), First Congregational Church, Saginaw (1867-1868), First Presbyterian Church, Three Rivers (1868-1870), First Baptist Church, Jackson (1868-1873), First United Methodist Church, Marquette (1871-1872), First Presbyterian Church, Marshall (1872-1873), and the First Congregational Church, Charlotte (1872-1876).

Summary Description

The First Congregational Church is a monumental brick Romanesque Revival building that was built in 1859-1860, and has a 1960-1961 two-story brick addition on its west elevation. The original building is clad with reddish brown brick, sits on a stone foundation, and is covered by an asphalt shingled gabled roof. The main mass of the church is rectangular in shape, but has a façade that projects out and extends about three-quarters of the way across the center portion of the building. The façade is dominated by two distinct towers on either side of a further projecting central entryway. The north end of the building is recessed on the east and west elevations, projects out from the building's main mass, and is covered with a gabled roof. The stained glass windows on the east and west elevations are original to the building, are of a grisaille style, and are interrupted by brick buttresses. All the windows on the original building have round heads. The sanctuary has a traditional auditorium plan with a raised chancel and rear gallery. The modern style two-story addition is constructed of brown brick with burgundy enameled metal panels, rests on a concrete foundation and has a flat roof. The addition's façade is noted for its ceramic tile "Alpha and Omega" mural.

The rear (north elevation) of the church is located on the corner of Pearl and Jackson Streets, and the façade (south elevation) faces the north end of Blackman Park. Blackman Park is the last remaining quarter of the public square which was platted at the four corners of the intersection of Jackson and Michigan Streets. When

[47]

originally constructed the First Congregational Church was located at the extreme west end of Jackson's downtown and easily stood higher than any nearby buildings. However, since then the downtown has extended to the west, and has surrounded the church. Taller buildings than the church were constructed in the 1920s, but the church maintains its massive feel.

North Elevation of Church, 2017
Photograph from the Author's Collection

Narrative Description

The First Congregational Church in Jackson, Michigan is a Romanesque Revival building constructed from 1859-1860. The majority of the building is constructed of reddish brown brick, rests on a coursed rock faced ashlar stone foundation and is covered with an asphalt shingled gabled roof. All the windows have tan limestone sills, but some are dark gray due to years of weathering. The windows at ground level are round arched with reddish brick rowlock headers, while the upper windows are round arched with tan brick rowlock headers. All elevations are capped by a simple bracketed wooden cornice.

Close-up View of Church Façade, 2017
Photograph from the Author's Collection

The central entryway projects out from the façade, is constructed of red brick, rests on a concrete water table, and is covered with a slate gabled roof. The entryway is at ground level with a recessed door and round arched stained glass window above, and topped by an arch formed with alternating rowlock and soldier brick courses.

The façade projects out from, and extends across approximately the central three-quarters of the main mass of the building. It is flanked by two distinct towers located at its east and west ends. The lower portion of both towers are symmetrical, but become different toward their tops. The west tower is shorter than the east tower, and is divided into two sections, while the east tower is

First Congregational Church Façade, 2017
South Elevation
Photograph from the Author's Collection

divided into four sections. The sections are framed with projecting brickwork at their corners, and divided by belt courses of tan limestone stonework. The lowest sections contain a set of paired windows with a single window above. This section is capped with a heavy tan brick corbel table. The second section contains a set of paired windows, and a tan brick framed quatrefoil window above. The differences in the east and west towers become apparent above the quatrefoil windows. The second section of the west tower is capped with a heavy pediment corbel table. The tower is covered with a four-sided sheet metal bell-cast roof with gabled dormers with a tan brick corbel table below. The third section of the east tower contains a series of three windows, and is topped with a tan brick corbel table. The highest section of the east tower houses the belfry with three windows with louvered openings. The center window is taller than the two side windows. This section is capped with a heavy corbel table below a cross face gabled slate roof. The corners of the roof contain brick piers which once supported decorative finials. The exposed east, west and north elevations of the two towers are similar in appearance to their respective south elevations. The center section of the façade is recessed slightly from the two tower fronts, with the roof from the building's main mass projecting between the towers. This section is located just above the entryway and contains a series of three windows with the center window being taller than the two side windows. A small round stone framed window is located above each of the three windows. The center section is finished with a corbel table that follows the rake of the gabled roof.

The east and west elevations of the original building are similar in appearance. These elevations are each divided into six sections. Each section contains a center round arch stained glass window with tan rowlock brick headers. Each section is flanked with stepped brick buttresses with smooth tan limestone offsets. A brick corbel table tops each section. The east elevation has an additional row of round arch windows at ground level that are aligned with the stained glass windows above. The north end of both elevations is set back and contains a set of upper and lower round arch serial windows. The roof at the north end of the building is lower than the roof's main mass. An upper door with a balconet on the east

East Elevation of Church, 2017
Photograph from the John Guidinger Collection

elevation is the original side entrance to the building before the building was raised and expanded.

The north elevation is divided into three sections. The narrow center section is bordered by projecting brick piers with three round arch windows arranged from bottom to top. The east and west sections are wider and also contain round arch windows arranged from bottom to top like the center section. The east section has two lower windows side by side where the west section has only one lower window.

Church Brickwork, 2017
West elevation of church looking east within courtyard.
Upper brickwork is the original church. Lower brickwork is the
1871 addition. Center rectangular areas show the location of
beams that supported the upper structure
when the building was raised in 1871.
Photograph from the Author's Collection

[53]

The color of the First Congregational Church brickwork shows the evidence of where the building has been altered. The brick color of the original structure is reddish brown, while the newer red brick on the lower part of the building shows where the 1871 addition was added. In addition, numerous rectangular bricked areas along the east and west elevations show where the wood beams were located which supported the building while it was raised during the 1871 addition. The red brick of the entryway on the south elevation is from the 1895 remodel of the entrance. The most recent modern addition on the west end of the building also has a different brown brick color.

Front of Church Sanctuary, 2017
Photograph from the Author's Collection

The interior of the church is accessed from the ground level entryway on the building's south elevation. Two sets of dogleg stairways ascend to the sanctuary which is entered through a center arched entryway. The sanctuary is rectangular in shape with plaster walls and a wood wainscot. The rear sanctuary wall has two non-functioning doorways which flank the center entryway. The doors and entryway have twisted rope round arch moldings. The gallery above has a solid wood balustrade with recessed round arch panels. Three large arches above the gallery reveal the stained glass windows on the front of the church.

Rear of Sanctuary, 2017
Photograph from the Author's Collection

The sanctuary has an auditorium plan with a center and two side aisles. The pews which are original to the building are in four sections with the side pews angled toward the chancel. The two center sections of pews are divided by a partition. The pews were originally constructed of butternut wood, but have since been stained walnut.

Typical Church Pew, 2017
Photograph from the Author's Collection

The chancel is a raised platform which is rectangular in shape and projects into the sanctuary. The front of the chancel is divided into thirds, with the center one-third projecting further into the sanctuary and a center half-round section extending beyond that. The recessed paneled wood work on the front of the chancel is similar to the woodwork on the front of the gallery. The chancel was originally constructed of oak, but has since been stained a dark walnut. A large archway spans the back of

Close-up view of Chancel, 2107
Photograph from the Author's Collection

the chancel with a simple molding above it. Seating for the choir is located under this archway and consists of wood pews on three steps. The back of the chancel has an ornate wood quatrefoil designed screen which was constructed in 1926 to hide the pipes of the organ. Although plans were proposed in 1936, 1958 and 1960 to redesign the chancel, none of the proposals were acted upon, and it retains its original look.

With the exception of the window in the southwest corner of the sanctuary, which was broken and replaced in the 1950s, the stained glass windows are original to the building. Each set of windows come with a pair of lower rectangular windows, and a pair of upper windows with rounded tops. The sections are separated by a wide vertical mullion and mid-level muntin. Each window has a center lozenge pattern of pinkish colored glass with a floral motif in the middle of each diamond shaped pane. The lozenge windows are similar on each window but are decorated with differing types of narrow borders adorned with repeating patterns of colored flowers and stems with solid backgrounds. One style of border contains white rounded flower petals and colored stems. Another border style contains flowers with squared white and yellow petals with white stems. Above and between the tops of each set of stained glass windows are small round stained glass medallions. Each medallion has a different design and all

Close-up view of Sanctuary Stained Glass, 2017
Photograph from the Author's Collection

have a religious meaning behind them. The medallions are the only religious ornamentation in the sanctuary.

The ceiling of the sanctuary is supported by large brackets located between each of the windows. The portion of the ceiling which is supported by the brackets angles upward at a low pitch toward the flat center. Two large round ornate medallions within square panels were constructed on the flat area of the ceiling. The medallions originally served as a means to vent hot air out the sanctuary during the summer months. The south medallion vented the air out to the west tower, and the north medallion vented the air out to the north end of the church. Both were closed when the church acquired air conditioning in 1999.

The ground floor of the building serves several social functions of the church. The largest room is the Fellowship Hall and it comprises approximately two-thirds of the ground floor space below the sanctuary. Smaller rooms like the library, Heritage Room, rest rooms, and lobby are located on the west end, and the kitchen and utility room are on the north end.

The modern 1960-1961 addition is two stories, rests on a concrete foundation and has a flat roof. The addition is in a "U" shape with an open court yard in the center. The main mass is a two-story L-shape, and is connected to the original church building by a one-story breezeway on the south side, and a second-story skyway on the north side. The façade of the addition has two recessed lower windows with an area of brickwork between. Above this is a modern ceramic tile mural called "Alpha and Omega." The mural has a green background with side by side yellow "A" and "Ω" symbols with alternating white

Fellowship Hall on Ground Level of Church, 2017
Photograph from the Author's Collection

circles repeated in a diagonal pattern. The west elevation of the addition is adorned with sections of burgundy enameled metal panels located above and below the second-story windows. The addition's north elevation second-story and skyway are also covered with the same burgundy enameled panels and metal framed windows. The breezeway on the south end of the addition is predominately enclosed in glass with burgundy enameled panels above and at ground level.

The courtyard within the addition is paved with four sections of concrete divided into strips which run in a north/south direction. These sections are framed with paver brick borders. The courtyard is entered from the

Courtyard Looking South, 2017
Photograph from the Author's Collection

north side along Pearl Street, under the second-story skyway. The skyway runs from the north end of the addition's second-story, to the recessed portion of the church's second-story west elevation. From within the courtyard the addition is entered through a door on the west end of the courtyard's south side. Both floors of the addition's west side contain classrooms that are connected without the use of a hallway. Offices are located on the south side of the first floor, and are connected by a hallway that leads to the one-story breezeway on its east end. The breezeway connects directly to the south end of the church's west elevation, and accesses the Fellowship Hall through a set of stairs. The breezeway can also be entered through a door on its south side.

The First Congregational Church retains a great deal of integrity. Besides the west addition, the exterior of the church has not changed since the front entrance was altered in 1895. The appearance of the sanctuary has gone through a number of changes, but mostly in paint colors, stenciling and different light fixtures. When the building was originally constructed the sanctuary was entered through a foyer which extended across the entire width of the building. The sanctuary could be entered through the center archway, but also through the two side doors which are now nonfunctioning. When the church was raised and added onto in 1871, the foyer and original entrance were retained, and the exterior steps to the entrance were expanded.

In 1895 when the front entrance was reconfigured the exterior steps were removed and the entrance was constructed at ground level. As part of the 1895 project the interior stairway to the sanctuary was constructed, the two doors flanking the center archway to the sanctuary were closed and plastered over on the stairway side. The lowest two sets of round arch windows on the south elevation of the two towers were added and new stained glass was added to the windows immediately above them and above the exterior doorway.

Finials once adorned the tops of both towers. The east tower contained finials at each corner, and at the apex of each gable. Historic photos show the finials on the east tower in a variety of states of disrepair throughout the history of the church. The finials were all removed from the east tower sometime between 1900 and the 1950s. The current finial on the west tower was once taller.

Bibliography

"1st Congregational To Break Ground." *Jackson Citizen Patriot* [Jackson, Michigan] 25 June 1960: 4. Print.

"An Old Landmark" *The American Citizen* [Jackson, Michigan] 21 Apr. 1859: Print.

Davey, Robert C. Bingham Memorial Organ, June 1976, Print.

DeLand, Charles V. *DeLand's History of Jackson County, Michigan Embracing a Concise Review of Its Early Settlement, Industrial Development and Present Conditions, Together with Interesting Reminiscences.* B.F. Bowen, 1903. Print.

Farmer, Silas. *History of Detroit and Wayne County and Early Michigan: A Chronological Cyclopedia of the Past and Present.* Detroit: Pub. by S. Farmer & for Munsell &, New York, 1890. Print.

Goodykoontz, Collin Brummitt. *Home Missions on the American Frontier: With Particular References to the American Home Missionary Society.* New York: Octagon, 1971. Print.

History of Jackson County, Michigan. Vol. 1. Chicago: Inter-state Pub., 1881. Print.

Horning, Elinore T. *Horatio Nelson White: The Man Who Changed the Face of Syracuse.* Mexico, NY: E. Horning, 1988. Print.

Jackson Citizen Patriot [Jackson, Michigan] 3 Nov. 1945: 3. Print.

"The Lifting of Chicago." *The Lifting of Chicago.*Web. 13 Feb. 2016. <http://users.ox.ac.uk/~sedm1912/lch.html>.

"Local Matters." *Jackson Daily Citizen* [Jackson, Michigan] 6 July 1871, Vol. VII ed., No. 88 Print.

--- *Jackson Daily Citizen* [Jackson, Michigan] 13 July 1871, Vol. VII ed., No. 94 Print.

--- *Jackson Daily Citizen* [Jackson, Michigan] 21 July 1871, Vol. VII ed., No. 101 Print.

--- *Jackson Daily Citizen* [Jackson, Michigan] 22 July 1871, Vol. VII ed., No. 102 Print.

--- *Jackson Daily Citizen* [Jackson, Michigan] 28 July 1871, Vol. VII ed., No. 107 Print.

--- *Jackson Daily Citizen* [Jackson, Michigan] 29 July 1871, Vol. VII ed., No. 108 Print.

--- *Jackson Daily Citizen* [Jackson, Michigan] 15 August 1871, Vol. VII ed., No. 122 Print.

--- *Jackson Daily Citizen* [Jackson, Michigan] 18 August 1871, Vol. VII ed., No. 125 Print.

--- *Jackson Daily Citizen* [Jackson, Michigan] 25 August 1871, Vol. VII ed., No. 131 Print.

--- *Jackson Daily Citizen* [Jackson, Michigan] 30 August 1871, Vol. VII ed., No. 135 Print.

--- *Jackson Daily Citizen* [Jackson, Michigan] 27 September 1871, Vol. VII ed., No. 159 Print.

--- *Jackson Daily Citizen* [Jackson, Michigan] 7 October 1871, Vol. VII ed., No. 168 Print.

--- *Jackson Daily Citizen* [Jackson, Michigan] 19 June 1895, Vol. XXXI ed., No. 73 Print.

--- *Jackson Daily Citizen* [Jackson, Michigan] 9 September 1895, Vol. XXXI ed., No. 132 Print.

--- *Jackson Daily Citizen* [Jackson, Michigan] 22 August 1899, Vol. XXXV ed., No. 102 Print.

--- *Jackson Daily Citizen* [Jackson, Michigan] 14 October 1899, Vol. XXXV ed., No. 168 Print.

--- *Jackson Daily Citizen* [Jackson, Michigan] 16 October 1899, Vol. XXXV ed., No. 169 Print.

Lingaur, Kenneth. National Register of Historic Places Nomination, First Congregational Church, Jackson Michigan. Sept. 2, 2016.

Meeks, Carroll L. V. "Romanesque before Richardson in the United States." *The Art Bulletin* 35.1 (1953): 17-33. Web.

"Old Timer Back, Church Bell Symphony Expanded." *Jackson Citizen Patriot* [Jackson, Michigan] 1954: Print.

Palmer, Jean, and Onondaga County Public Library. "James Morwick." Message to Marilyn Guidinger 2 Dec. 2004. E-mail.

Parsons, Gerald J. "Horatio N White." Letter. 5 May 1976. MS. Onandaga Public Library, Syracuse, New York.

"Redecoration Week at the First Congregational Church." *Jackson Citizen Patriot* [Jackson, Michigan] 7 Oct. 1923: Print.

Sampson, Claude DeWitt. Membership Files. The American Institute of Architects Archives. The AIA Historical Directory of American Architects: ahd1039008. Web.18 March. 2016

Sanborn Fire Insurance Map. *Environmental Data Resources*: Sanborn Map Company, Pelham, NY, Jackson MI. 1899. Sheets 7. Print

---. *Environmental Data Resources*: Sanborn Map Company, Pelham, NY, Jackson MI. 1907. Sheet 28. Print.

---. *Environmental Data Resources*: Sanborn Map Company, Pelham, NY, Jackson MI. 1930. Vol 1. Sheet 1. Print.

Steege, Gwen W. "The 'Book of Plans' and the Early Romanesque Revival in the United States: A Study in Architectural Patronage." Journal of the Society of Architectural Historians 46.3 (1987): 215-27. Web.

Taylor, Richard H. *The Plan of Union in Michigan*. 1992. MS. Benton Harbor, MI.

"The New Congregational Church " *The American Citizen* [Jackson, Michigan] 1 Sept. 1859: Print.

The Traverse Region, Historical and Descriptive: With Illustrations of Scenery and Portraits and Biographical Sketches of Some of its Prominent Men and Pioneers: Chicago: H.R. Page, 1884. Print.

United States. Department of Interior. National Park Service. *National Register of Historic Places Nomination, First Congregational Church, Charlotte, Michigan*. By Robert O. Christensen and Charles C. Cotman. Lansing, Michigan: 1993. Print.

Drawing of the First Congregational Church, 1886
From the Sanborn Fire Insurance Map Company
Pelham, New York

About the Author

Kenneth Lingaur is a native of Northern Michigan. He spent his early years in Lake Leelanau, Michigan, and has lived in Clare, Michigan since 2003. He earned his Master's Degree in Historic Preservation from Eastern Michigan University in 2014, and the following year founded Lingaur Preservation LLC.

Lingaur Preservation LLC is a historic preservation consulting firm specializing in the research and documentation of historic places.

Ken got his first taste of Jackson's history while writing the National Register of Historic Places Nomination for the First Congregational Church. The church was listed on the National Register in 2017.

Ken Lingaur has been married since 1995, and along with his wife, Sherrie, have four boys.

For more information on Lingaur Preservation LLC visit his website at www.lingaurpreservation.com.

Other Books by Kenneth Lingaur

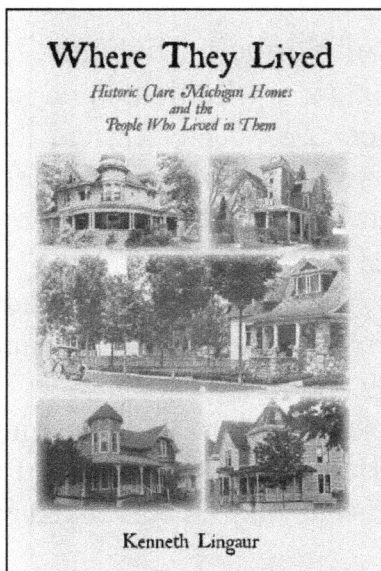

Where They Lived
Historic Clare Michigan Homes and the People Who Lived in Them

Kenneth Lingaur

Clare, Michigan may seem like your ordinary Midwest town, but some of the people that lived here were far from usual. In these pages you will read about a man who was ship wrecked in the middle of the Atlantic Ocean, a couple who missed their trip to America on the Titanic, a man who came to Clare with nothing and became her most famous citizen, and what story about Clare would be complete without gangsters.

Where They Lived chronicles the lives of the people who lived in fifty-one historic Clare homes. After reading this book you will see these houses in a new light, and hopefully appreciate the history behind them.

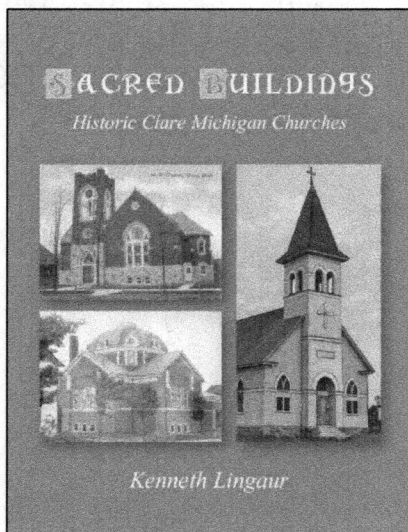

SACRED BUILDINGS
Historic Clare Michigan Churches

Kenneth Lingaur

From simple wood frame buildings to a church listed on the National Register of Historic Places, the church buildings in Clare, Michigan are varied.

Spanning from the founding of Clare to the present *Sacred Buildings: Historic Clare Michigan Churches* tells the story of seventeen different church buildings from thirteen congregations.

This is the story of the places that the people of Clare built to share their common faith and worship their God.

Sacred Buildings: Historic Clare Michigan Churches is full of photographs and descriptions which take you inside many of these buildings.

These books are available at Amazon.com and local Clare, Michigan retailers